Following the Derwent

JULIE BUNTING

" the Derwent is a frightful creature when the hills load her current with water; I say, we kept our distance, and contented ourselves with hearing the roaring of its waters ... "

Defoe (1726)

SHEFFIELD • ENGLAND • 2004

PART ONE

Ladybower to Hathersage

Nearly half the population of England lives within 60 miles of the River Derwent, which follows a southerly course through the Peak District and is contained entirely within Derbyshire. The infant river gathers amongst the rocks and peat of Swains Greave (SK128974) between Bleaklow and the Howden Moors. Lesser rivers join the Derwent along its route, including the Noe at Bamford, the Wye at Rowsley, the Amber at Ambergate and the Ecclesbourne at Duffield. All have taken turns at driving mill machinery, playing a vital role in Britain's industrial progress. The Derwent Valley between Matlock Bath and Derby holds World Heritage Site status for its international importance as birthplace of the factory system.

Glover, writing around 1830 in the *Derbyshire Gazetteer*, calls the Derwent 'the chief of our native rivers' and gives this geologist's-eye view of its course: 'Numerous minor springs and streamlets, which when surcharged with rain become torrents, unite with this principal or eastern water-head, and at a small town called Derwent, the waters constitute a rapid river. The bed of this river, from its source until it approaches Matlock, is chiefly gritstone and shale; but from the foot of the High Tor to Cromford Bridge, it flows over the alternations of limestone and toadstone strata ... From

Cromford to some miles below Belper, the bed of the stream is chiefly gritstone rock and grit shale, and then until within about a mile of Derby, it intersects some wide deposits of quartz-gravel and limestone shale. The remainder of its course until its junction with the Trent near the village of Wilne, is through red marl, sandy quartz-gravel, and patches of limestone rock'.

Drowned Villages

The Derwent used to have a well-earned reputation for flooding with little warning, and its course is littered with stories of lives lost. One tragedy has gone down in legend as the Maid of Derwent, a 17th-century romance ending with the sad fate of Mistress Annie Moreton. Annie was eloping with her lover but drowned while crossing the swollen river, possibly over the stepping stones at Hathersage. An anonymous poet brought the tale to an end:

> *'To cross the mountain's headlong stream*
> *They stepped from stone to stone;*
> *They slipped, alas! – and then a scream*
> *Waked darkness on her throne.*
> *Into the flood sweet Annie sank,*
> *Death's pangs, ah! soon were o'er;*
> *To her the past became a blank;*
> *A vision now no more.'*

Three centuries on, the river was reined in to feed three new reservoirs in the Upper Derwent Valley – the Howden, Derwent and Ladybower. The first two were completed in 1916, built with 1.25 million tons of stone transported on a specially-built railway. The track-bed is now the Thornhill Trail, a footpath along the eastern foot of Win Hill, but the actual track was taken up during the First World War and relaid on the Western Front for transporting troops.

During construction of the Howden and Derwent, between 1901-1915, over 2,700 navvies and their families lived in the temporary village of Birchinlee, otherwise known as 'Tin Town'. Houses were provided for families and bunkhouses for single men, as well as a hospital, canteen, shops, school, public baths and allotments. It is still possible to trace the remains of cobbled streets and shanty houses.

The two 'real' villages of Derwent and Ashopton had to be forfeited for the third reservoir, Ladybower, constructed between 1935-45. Displaced villagers were rehoused in a new settlement at Yorkshire Bridge while their old homes passed into memory as the 'drowned villages'. For many years the spire of the church of St James and St John poked out of the water. During the severe droughts of 1959 and 1989, hundreds of visitors re-trod the roads of Derwent village, marked out by remnants of stone walls standing in the sun-baked mud. The ancient Derwent packhorse bridge, however, can still be seen intact. It was dismantled stone by stone and rebuilt at the head of the valley at Slippery Stones, in memory of Sheffield rambler and author John Derry.

The Upper Derwent region, where life is still concentrated on sheep farming, became part of Britain's first national park at its designation in 1951. Derwent Valley Water Board was incorporated into Severn Trent Water in 1974. In total the three reservoirs cover a six-mile expanse of water, with trout fishing on the Ladybower and Derwent in season, and rowing boats for hire by fishermen. Impressive cascades gush down the dam walls at certain times of year; since 2000, visitors have been able to walk across the Ladybower wall.

Ladybower is the final destination of the pretty River Alport, having made its lonely moorland descent past Alport Castles Farm. For over two-and-a-half centuries the annual Methodist Love Feast has been held in this isolated spot. Here too was born suffragette Hannah Mitchell who campaigned with the Pankhursts.

The A57 climbs westwards to reach almost 1,700ft (518m) at the Snake Pass, notorious for quickly becoming impassable in times of snow. In the opposite direction, a no-through road leaves the A57 for Derwent Reservoir, with parking places and a cycle hire centre at Fairholmes, giving access to a cycle trail beside the reservoir. Proposals are under way for charging motorists to use the no-through road during busy periods, both to ease traffic congestion and to protect the environment. The section of road beyond Fairholmes is already closed to motor vehicles on Sundays throughout the summer.

Beside Derwent Reservoir stands a monument detailing the devoted vigil of Tip, a sheepdog. Her master was an old Derwent shepherd who lost his life on the moors 50 years ago, his body guarded by Tip until they were found 15 weeks later, the dog barely alive.

During the Second World War the Derwent dams were used for practice runs by Lancaster Bombers of 617 Squadron, perfecting their use of the 'bouncing bombs' which breached the Ruhr Valley dams of industrial Germany in 1943. Thus were born the Dambusters, commemorated in a plaque and memorial museum in the west tower of Derwent Dam (for opening times check with Fairholmes Visitor Centre, 01433 650953).

Pins and Needles

Leaving the reservoirs behind, the river flows on to Bamford. The remains of Peaklanders buried at the old 'drowned' church of Derwent village were re-interred in Bamford churchyard.

In times past, the River Derwent ran unhindered from its source until it was put to work turning the waterwheel of Bamford corn mill. In 1782 this became a cotton mill operated by a local farmer and miller. Other uses followed into modern times but Bamford Mill has finally done with industry; the handsome building is now residential accommodation.

The Derwent absorbs the River Noe just beyond Brough, site of the Roman fort of Navio, an atmospheric place though there is little left to see. Next major settlement on the river is Hathersage, where the stepping stones referred to earlier mark the ancient crossing of several packhorse routes. In the 1800s Hathersage was a smoky, dust-laden place, its chief industries wire-drawing and the manufacture of needles and pins. The worst job was grinding points on needles, work which took years off the operators' lives.

Hathersage has a close connection with Charlotte Brontë through her friendship with Ellen Nussey, sister to the vicar of Hathersage. Charlotte stayed at the vicarage in 1845, alighting from her stagecoach at The George. She used Hathersage as her model for Morton in *Jane Eyre* and took her heroine's surname from a local family. North Lees Hall became the fictional Thornfield Hall, home of Mr Rochester. According to tradition, North Lees is one of seven local halls built in the 15th century by Robert Eyre, one for each of his sons.

The real Eyre family settled in the Peak in Norman times. Legend tells that their surname was bestowed by William, Duke of Normandy at the Battle of Hastings. William had been knocked from his horse and was lying winded on the ground with his visor jammed shut when a soldier rushed to remove the dented helmet, saving the Duke from suffocation. The man gave his name as Truelove but William declared that he should henceforth be known as Air or Eyre since he had given him air to breathe. The soldier returned to the fray and was severely wounded with the loss of a leg. After the battle William, now the Conqueror, heard of his rescuer's bravery and rewarded him with generous gifts of land and the right to a crest showing a disembodied armour-clad leg. Several beautiful memorial brasses to the Eyres can be seen in the church of St Michael and All Angels, Hathersage.

Hathersage Church, from Highways & Byways of Derbyshire.

6

PART TWO

Hathersage to Baslow

Hathersage churchyard is firmly on the tourist trail as the site of Little John's grave. When the grave was opened in 1784 it revealed the remains of a man who in life had been a good seven feet tall. Legend has it that Little John was born in Hathersage and at the end of his life came home to die in the cottage where he had been born. Coincidence or not, the name of England's favourite outlaw lives on in Robin Hood's Cave on Stanage Edge – acclaimed by rock climbers as the finest training ground in the country – Robin Hood's Well in Longshaw Country Park and two hamlets named Robin Hood near Baslow and Whatstandwell. Furthermore, Hood's Brook runs through Hathersage; it used to power some of the wire-drawing mills referred to earlier.

Beside the Derwent at Hathersage is a private residence named Leadmill. Whilst it may have connections with the lead industry, its earlier history places it as a corn mill and it seems to have ended its working life as a stonemason's yard, using water power for sawing and dressing stone. Padley Mill, once powered by the Burbage Brook on its way to the Derwent, is another private house occupying a former corn mill; this too eventually became a sawmill.

Hathersage, with its shops, eateries and outdoor swimming pool, is a popular stop-off point between visitor attractions in the Hope Valley and the Dark Peak. Winding on towards Grindleford, the Derwent bypasses The Round House, the distinctive cutlery factory of David Mellor. Designed by Sir Michael Hopkins and hailed as a minor masterpiece of modern architecture, the building stands on the site of a former gasworks. The circular gas-holder foundation suggested the design of the factory, completed in 1990 of local gritstone, overhung by a circular lead roof. The Round House has won a number of major awards and was voted one of Britain's most outstanding buildings of the 20th century.

Further downstream is Grindleford Bridge, where a 17th-century highwayman had a narrow escape from the law. William Nevison, known as 'Bold Nevison', was in the area for the unlikely purpose of repaying a victim whom he had held up and robbed. His escapade at Grindleford followed a busy day stealing purses at Bakewell market, where he almost got caught. He was pursued as far as Grindleford Bridge. There he tried to keep out of sight by walking his horse through the river, only to be spotted and fired upon by the night watchman. Nevison returned the shot as he headed for the safety of Padley Woods. He afterwards extended his area of operations but his luck didn't hold and he was executed at York on 4 May 1684.

The Derwent flows on through Froggatt, overlooked by Froggatt Edge with its stone circle and rocky ascents so often dotted with brightly-helmeted rock climbers. The skies above are the haunt of hang gliders and also winged gliders making leisurely manoeuvres above their club base at Camphill. Riverbank footpaths follow the Derwent beyond Froggatt Bridge to continue past the old and new bridges of Calver, with Calver Edge taking over the eastern skyline from Froggatt Edge. The old Calver Bridge, which carried the turnpike road from East Moor to Wardlow Mires, suffered the familiar fate of nearly all Derwent bridges when it was swept away by a raging flood in August 1799.

Swastika and Plastic Cobbles

Local place names give some idea of Calver's varied industrial past: Calver Sough and the Brightside and Red Rake Soughs – lead mining; Stocking Farm – textiles; and Mill Farm – which stands close to where the river was put to work at a corn mill. Calver Mill, now converted into residential apartments, was built as a cotton mill in 1778, replacing a water-powered corn mill. The building was badly damaged by the flood of 1799 and three years later burned to the ground. It was succeeded by a much larger seven-storey mill with fireproof cast-iron pillars. Cotton continued to be produced until 80 years ago, then a smaller building at the rear became a jam factory, kept supplied with lorry loads of turnips from local farms. Fire struck again in 1937 and the building became a fluorspar washing plant. After the war the semi-derelict mill was taken over by W & G Sissons of Sheffield for the manufacture of stainless steel sinks and kitchen equipment.

In the 1970s Calver Mill became nationally famous as Schloss Colditz – Colditz Castle – in a television series. Work at Sissons was suspended, the mill yard was laid with plastic

cobbles and from time to time 'escaping POWs' could be spotted running across the roof of the mill with their heads down. 'German soldiers' were seen at Curbar Gap and a swastika flew from the factory roof. The flag was still flying when the Duke of Windsor died, and a man who had seen it as he drove through Calver complained to a national newspaper, denouncing the bad taste of flying a swastika in connection with the Duke's death.

Once under the road bridge, the Derwent swings away from the main A623 but then river and road meet up again almost opposite Cliff College, a training centre for Methodist ministers. Its near neighbour, Grislowfields Farm, brings to mind a sad story about the family who died here when plague broke out in 1632. It took the lives of Thomas Cundy, his wife Ada and their three children. Together they lie buried on open land below the northerly slopes of Baslow Edge, their graves marked by five stone slabs carved with their initials.

The Cundy Plague Graves

Coming within sight of Baslow, the Derwent curves into Bubnell, a pretty hamlet with a Hall, an overgrown pinfold and a history of framework knitting and hat making. Baslow has its Hall too, now a restaurant on the main road. Ninety years ago the property became home to Sebastian de Ferranti, a pioneering inventor in the field of electrical engineering. He equipped

Baslow Bridge defied the floods

Baslow Hall with fittings ahead of their time: central heating from radiators fixed to the ceilings, wireless sets in every room, an all-electric laundry, floodlighting and an electric lawn mower. An electrically heated egg-laying plant was abandoned when the hens received a nasty, fatal, shock.

Back on the river, downstream below the weir, was once Hodgkinson's corn mill and bakehouse, its waterwheel removed about 70 years ago. The old stone bridge at Baslow is thought to be the only Derwent bridge in the Peak to have defied the floods. It has stood firm for some four centuries. A tiny, quaint building known as the watchman's hut or toll house stands on the bridge. Here a watch was kept to prevent heavy loads, especially millstones, being carried over the bridge without payment of a toll.

Surely no church stands closer to the Derwent than St Anne's at Baslow, its churchyard reaching right up to the riverbank. Several curiosities catch the visitor's eye, not least one face of the church clock. Erected to commemorate Queen Victoria's diamond jubilee, the face is encircled with VICTORIA 1897 instead of the usual 12 numerals. The base

of a sanctuary knocker survives on the south door of the church, the goal of bygone fugitives seeking refuge from the law. St Anne's also has a dog whip of ashwood and leather, formerly used by the parish dog whipper to drive troublesome dogs from church during services. In days gone by, people regularly took their dogs to church, perhaps for the walk, and some dogs must have preferred a scrap to a sermon. As for Baslow's font, the story goes that for a time it was used to salt the vicar's bacon!

Baslow Bridge Toll House

9

PART THREE

Baslow to Rowsley

The Derwent is barely out of Baslow before it enters Chatsworth Park. Two fisheries along the river are managed from Chatsworth Estate Office and keepered by three water bailiffs. The Derwent harbours natural brown and rainbow trout and contains a good head of grayling, with just over four miles of fishing on both banks, from the old bridge at Baslow, on through the park and ending at Smelting Mill Brook north of Rowsley.

When the 4th Duke of Devonshire (1720-64) made sweeping changes to the park, a channel was cut across an S-bend in the Derwent upstream of the House. This set the river on a straighter course and solved the problem of intermittent flooding. Walpole had earlier written that 'the river runs before the door, and serpentizes more than you can conceive'.

At that time Edensor village straggled as far as the river, well within sight of the House. When

'…the river runs before the door…'

Paine's Upstream Bridge, Chatsworth

James Paine was engaged by the 4th Duke to build the new 'one arch' bridge, he removed a mill and some cottages. Seventy years later, the 6th Duke and Joseph Paxton had the rest of the village demolished and rebuilt Edensor as it is now. A well-known story tells how the two men chose different designs from the architect's pattern book, so that no two houses are the same, 'from the sturdy Norman to the sprightly Italian'. One house was spared because it was home to an old man whom the kindly Duke refused to disturb, and there it remains, all alone in its walled garden almost opposite the gates to Edensor.

The 7th Duke employed Sir Gilbert Scott to enlarge the 14th-century church of St Peter, which contains a memorial brass to Paxton and the remarkable tomb of two sons of Bess of Hardwick. On the opposite wall hangs a faded circlet of everlasting flowers sent by Queen Victoria on the assassination of Lord Frederick Cavendish in 1882. His funeral procession through Chatsworth Park was attended by a quarter of a million mourners. The Cavendish burial plot in the churchyard contains unassuming family graves including that of

Kathleen Kennedy, sister of President John F. Kennedy. Kathleen, who died in an air crash in 1948, was the widow of the present Duke's elder brother, Billy Hartington, killed by a sniper in the Second World War.

Edensor, Pilsley and Beeley are known as the three estate villages. Edensor has the church and a post office, but for a school and a pub – and the renowned Chatsworth Farm Shop – you have to go to Pilsley. Good news for 2004 is the opening of a village store and tea shop at Beeley, where the last village shop closed some years ago. Shortly before the Derwent flows out of Chatsworth Park it passes the impressive shell of Paine's mid-18th-century corn mill. The mill still has some machinery, a waterwheel, and a millstone propped against the outer wall, while the head- and tail-races can still be traced. The mill ground corn for animal feedstuffs until 1952 but ten years later was severely damaged by two beech trees brought down during a dreadful storm. Writes the Duchess of Devonshire in *The Estate A View from Chatsworth*: 'Knock it down,' they said. 'Don't knock it down, leave it as a ruin,' said Tony Snowdon, who was staying with us when its fate was being discussed. Leave it we did ... '

Traffic entering or leaving the south end of the park crosses the Derwent over the humped One Arch Bridge. Walkers have to negotiate the 'kissing stiles' and may well spot a strange contraption suspended beneath the bridge: a barrier of chains and poles intended to prevent deer from swimming out of bounds.

River and road now make towards Beeley, to be joined by Beeley Brook as it completes its journey from the moors via a sequence of leaps, twists and waterfalls in the oddly-named Hell Bank Plantation. An endlessly popular spot for walkers and picnickers, the woodland is bounded by a path giving access to the prehistoric monument of Hob Hurst's House on Beeley Moor. Thomas Bateman excavated this tumulus in 1853, revealing the remains of human bones 'lying in the very spot where they had been drawn together while embers of the funeral pyre were glowing'.

Various packhorse ways seem to have crossed paths at Hob Hurst's House and a number of early stone guide posts stand on the surrounding moorland. Lead smelting once took place on Beeley Edge and millstone grit was extracted from numerous quarries on Beeley Moor, now camouflaged by nature and time.

Swimming and Skating

Down in Beeley village is a pub, a lovely old church and, at the time of writing, a village shop nearing completion. Before the days of Beeley village hall, special gatherings such as the annual horticultural show were held in what is now known as Duke's Barn. Shire horses from Chatsworth Estate were once stabled in this building too but by the 1970s it no longer had any agricultural use. The Very Reverend R. A. Beddoes, Vicar of Edensor and Chairman of the Board of the Royal School for the Deaf in Derby, proposed converting the barn into a residential centre where young deaf people could take part in outdoor activities and field studies. Thanks to a long-term free tenure given by the Duke of Devonshire and Chatsworth Settlement Trustees, the Duke's Barn Countryside Centre opened for this very purpose in May 1987.

Back on the main road, travellers can keep the Derwent in sight all the way to Rowsley. For over two miles the river serves as the boundary of the Peak District National Park. En route it separates Great Rowsley from Little Rowsley, respectively west and east of the river, though few people make the distinction nowadays. On the far side of Rowsley the River Wye loses its independence to join the Derwent. Generations of village children have learnt to

swim in one or other of the two rivers, but it is the Derwent which is remembered for freezing over for ice skating. The final task of the Wye is to turn the turbines of Caudwell's Mill. Through the vision and efforts of volunteers, the old machinery of this fascinating building, built in 1874, still produces strong wholemeal flour. Better still, the mill is open to visitors. A restaurant and craft workshops are housed in the stables and outbuildings.

Rowsley Station, however, its passenger platforms and goods yards once a hive of activity, is no more. Known as the company with the longest name and the shortest line, the Manchester, Buxton, Matlock and Midland Junction Railway opened between Ambergate and Rowsley in 1849. From Rowsley a choice of two possible onward routes were considered, one past Haddon Hall and the other through Chatsworth Park. The Duke of Rutland was opposed to the Haddon route but the 6th Duke of Devonshire, encouraged by Joseph Paxton, actively supported the idea of bringing the railway through Chatsworth. He subscribed £50,000 to the project and the great George Stephenson planned a tunnel under Park Wood. At the last minute the Duke of Rutland, lobbied by Bakewell tradesmen and attracted by the promise of generous compensation for disturbance, changed his mind. He did, however, insist that no evidence of the railway should be visible from Haddon Hall, so the track was laid through a tunnel and cutting. The tunnel collapsed during construction with the loss of several lives, commemorated in a memorial close to Rowsley church porch.

In 1863 the first trains steamed in and out of Rowsley, an important goods and passenger link in the growing national rail network. A survivor from those early railway days is the delightful station building designed by Joseph Paxton. It is now the centrepiece of Peak Village, a retail shopping complex.

PART FOUR

Rowsley to Matlock

Until the 'Beeching Axe' fell in the 1960s, the main railway line kept close company with the Derwent for many miles south of Rowsley. Peak Rail – of which more later – has its sights firmly set on re-laying the track between Matlock and Buxton. The society has so far restored the line as far as Rowsley, passing the site of sidings where stone from the highly-regarded Stancliffe Quarries was once loaded onto railway wagons tons at a time. The quarries lie behind Stancliffe Hall, home to Sir

Joseph Whitworth (1803-87) for the last 15 years of his life.

Whitworth was one of the most significant inventors of the Industrial Revolution, responsible for the standard screw thread, standardised gauges, the Whitworth rifle and a rifled cannon. He showed 20 products at the Great Exhibition of 1851, winning a record number of awards including a gold medal for a measuring device accurate to one-millionth of an inch. Income from Whitworth's estate gave

The 'Warrington' at Peak Rail's Darley Station

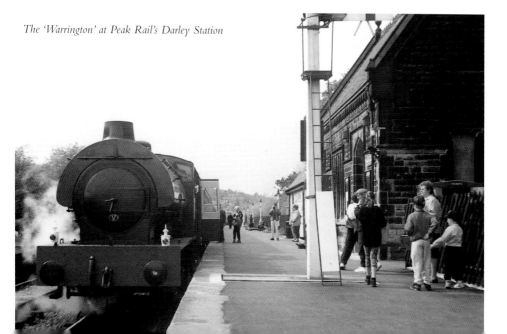

Darley Dale a cottage hospital, an exceptionally grand village institute and the lovely Whitworth Park – all three still in regular use. Sir Joseph and Lady Whitworth are buried side by side in St Helen's churchyard, Darley Dale, almost within shade of the famous Darley yew, one of the most ancient trees in the country at around 2,000 years old.

Early records tell how the Derwent frequently burst its banks and flooded right up to the churchyard, sometimes bringing with it great sheets of ice. Floods also played havoc with Darley Bridge. A 17th-century reference mentions a seven-arched bridge at this important river crossing but now only five are visible. The two pointed arches are original while the three semi-circular ones date from a widening of the upstream side of the bridge. Parish registers refer to a number of lives lost in the river through one reason or another.

For six weeks in 1904 the people of Darley Dale and Matlock were disturbed by the 'Mystery of the Missing Hand' after reports that a human hand had been seen in the Derwent. Police dragged the river from Darley to Matlock for three days without result. When a cricket glove was found near the river bank, the mystery was considered solved.

The road from Darley Bridge climbs to the old lead mining villages of Wensley and Winster, passing in the distance the seemingly castellated outline of Robin Hood's Stride, a natural gritstone outcrop also known as Mock Beggar's Hall. Winster is one of the most picturesque villages in the Peak, with winding gennels, quaint gritstone cottages and a historic market house. A further climb from Winster reaches Elton, an exposed village renowned as a bit of a ski resort when it snows properly.

A minor road from Stanton Moor and Stanton Lees also emerges at Darley Bridge. Surrounded by working quarries, Stanton Moor is an important Bronze Age landscape scattered with burial cairns and stone circles. Several footpaths lead to the distinctive Nine Ladies stone circle with its outlying King Stone. The moor is associated with the Beaker People, so-called from the pottery urns found in their burial places.

Below Stanton Lees lies Enthovens lead recycling works, successor to the mighty Mill Close mine, the greatest lead mine the country has ever known. Its most profitable era peaked in the 1930s, when the Duke of Rutland's royalties reportedly averaged £800 per week. At that time the most up-to-date machinery was draining previously inaccessible depths, keeping 400 miners in shift work, seven days and seven nights a week. Towards the end, in 1938, 5,550 gallons of water per minute were being raised, pouring into the Derwent via the Yatestoop Sough. (A sough is a man-made adit or drainage tunnel.)

Winster Market House

The Oker Sycamore Tree

Further up-river is the sough tail of the record-breaking Hillcar Sough. Hillcar was driven between 1766 and 1787 to give deeper drainage to the Alport lead mines. At four-and-a-half miles it was the longest sough in Derbyshire. This subterranean waterway was partly navigable by flat-bottomed boats; the boatmen were paid 1s 2d per day (6p), compared with a miner's pay of 1s (5p).

Many Mill Close miners came from Two Dales, originally called Toadhole. In spite of present-day appearances this pretty village has a long history of quarrying and milling. Johnson's East Mill, which today produces animal feeds, is successor to a series of industries which utilised the deceptively small Warney Brook, yet another tributary of the Derwent. The brook is fed by a series of dams hidden deep in Ladygrove Woods below Sydnope Hall.

For 30 years from 1827 Sydnope Hall was the seat of Sir Francis Sacheverell Darwin, son of Erasmus Darwin by his second marriage. By his first marriage Erasmus was grandfather to the renowned evolutionist Charles Darwin.

Warney Brook flows on to join the Derwent and a scene now opens up of low-lying meadows, where recent floodings have deceived the eye into thinking that the Peak occasionally has a Lake District. It all looked most impressive from the lofty summit of Oker Hill with its landmark tree, once the inspiration for Wordsworth. In his sonnet *The Keepsake*, two brothers each plant a sycamore on top of the hill before going their separate ways. One man met with success and his tree flourished, but his brother was a failure and his sycamore grew ever weaker and died.

By Coach and by Steam

Peak Rail trains now steam along between the river and the A6, passing beneath Old Road, home to the Red House Working Carriage Museum. This large collection of horse-drawn vehicles and equipment includes one of the very few surviving Hansom Cabs, a stage coach, a Royal Mail coach and carriages which have starred on television and in films from *Peak Practice* to *Sons and Lovers, The Virgin and the Gypsy, Chitty-Chitty-Bang-Bang, Jane Eyre, Pride and Prejudice* and *Sense and Sensibility*. Owner of the museum is Caroline Dale-Leech, the only woman ever to win the Coach Horn Competition at the Royal Show. Her horse-drawn carriages, often with Caroline at the reins, are a familiar sight on local roads, carrying lucky trippers to Chatsworth, Haddon Hall and further afield.

Matlock is the next port of call for the Derwent, first passing close to the run-down Cawdor Quarry area which is earmarked for extensive regeneration. From here a public footpath, the river, the A6 and the Peak Rail line all head straight into town, a dead end as far as the mainline from Derby is concerned. This is where the axe fell. And so it would have remained but for Peak Rail, a volunteer body formed in 1975 with a pledge to re-open the 20-mile mainline route between Matlock and Buxton. A loan stock issue raised £47,000 and the first lengths of track were laid at either end of the proposed line. Peak Rail is unique amongst private railways in having rail links at each terminus, thus offering access to the main rail network in both directions. The reinstated line from Matlock has already revitalised Darley Dale station and continues as far as Rowsley South, with steam trains running to a year-round timetable.

Matlock mainline station played an important role during the town's world famous hydropathic era, pioneered by mill owner John Smedley. His massive hydro, now County Hall, is a major landmark on the Matlock skyline. Overlooking the town from the south, in an even more elevated position at 850ft above sea level, is the brooding shell of Smedley's former home, Riber Castle.

Countless thousands of invalids and trippers have alighted at Matlock station, and countless tons of stone have been despatched from here. Quarry owners and stone merchants once had extensive wharves in the station yard, with scores of masons at work dressing stone largely destined for overseas. Matlock millstones were sent to grind wood pulp for paper manufacturers in Norway, the USA and the colonies; building stone was exported to Australia; and fine grindstones quarried at Tansley produced needles, glass stoppers, cutlery and files.

A hundred years ago Matlock's medieval bridge over the Derwent was widened, revealing the original packhorse bridge within the masonry. Built for slow, horse-drawn traffic, and without footpaths, the later bridge had become a bottleneck for vehicles and pedestrians alike. It also suffered from the immense weight of carts carrying stone from the quarries to the station. At present the bridge is being considered for pedestrianisation.

Matlock Old Bridge

16

From the bridge the Derwent flows unhindered through Hall Leys Park, given to the town in 1898 by Henry Knowles as a 'public promenade and pleasure resort for ever'. Surrounded by flower beds on Park Head is the Victorian clock tower and old tram shelter, moved here after Matlock's cable tramway closed in 1927. At the other end of the park a miniature railway runs along the riverbank, passing close to the stone memorial to a policeman who drowned trying to save a young woman who had jumped into the river.

The Derwent is now joined by Bentley Brook, which on its gradual descent from Matlock Moor once powered a sequence of mills in Lumsdale, from bleachworks and dyeworks to smallware (haberdashery) and a tape and shawl factory which exported worldwide. Lumsdale is now conserved as an important archaeological site but also has great natural beauty: steeply wooded slopes, waterfalls, rocky outcrops and high expanses of bracken.

Bentley Brook enters the Derwent close to where Hall Leys Park borders onto Causeway Lane, a main road named after the early causeway of huge stone slabs that carried wheeled traffic across the then waterlogged meadows. A large expanse of land had to be drained and cleared before the modern shops could be built at the bottom of Firs Parade. The Derwent made matters worse by regularly bursting its banks and Matlock town centre has been flooded many times within living memory. Flood prevention measures seem to have tamed the river but it still has enough life in it to attract competitors to the traditional Boxing Day raft races. Anything goes as long as it floats, with scores of weird and wonderful craft attempting the voyage down river to Matlock Bath.

Matlock, flooded in 1907

PART FIVE

Matlock to Cromford

As the Derwent passes through Matlock Dale it becomes a feature of one of the most photographed, sketched and painted scenes in England. Artists' Corner speaks for itself, with its whitewashed cottages following the curve of road and river below High Tor. This spectacular limestone outcrop, almost 400ft high, drew wonderment from early

High Tor, 'kissing the very heavens'

travellers. In *Gem of the Peak* (1843) William Adam enthused over its 'towering majesty ... kissing the very heavens to mingle with the stars'. The exposed sheer slopes of High Tor are an irresistible challenge to climbers but it has a sad history of accidents when people have scrambled too close to the edge.

High Tor and its grounds make up one of seven parks in the ongoing Matlock Parks Project. Access to the grounds is free but not so long ago there was a charge to ramble on High Tor and explore the Roman and Fern caves – damp, deep fissures left by the outcropping of lead veins. Many people still expect to see the distinctive wooden refreshment room but it burnt down in the 1990s.

Down in the Dale the Swiss chalet-style buildings of Matlock Bath railway station are reborn as the attractive Whistlestop Centre, run by Derbyshire Wildlife Trust as a wildlife exhibition centre and gift shop. The nearby cable car base station despatches its gondolas to swing dizzyingly upwards and over the Derwent gorge to the Heights of Abraham. Amongst the attractions up here is the Victoria Prospect Tower and two show caves. Great Rutland cavern is a former lead mine and has been open to visitors for nearly 200 years.

There is much to tell about the extraction of lead and other minerals in the Peak and this is the raison d'être of the very 'hands-on' Peak District Mining Museum at Matlock Bath. A visit can be combined with a trip down Temple Mine, where quite respectable samples of gold have been found. The museum itself has gone a long way to giving a new lease of life to the

Grand Pavilion, in fact the recently painted building is now, quite literally, in the pink.

The fishpond and fountain outside the Pavilion are fed by the thermal waters which gave Matlock Bath its very name as a famous spa. Old photographs of the fishpond show slot machines on the railings, where a penny bought a small box of fish food, such as dried grubs and shrimps. The council paid a tanner (2.5p) each for wasps' nests; these and their grubs were broken up and packaged for the machines. Built into the right-hand wall of the fishpond, as seen from the front, is a barely legible underwater milestone dated 1801. It originally stood further back but was re-sited beside the then clay-bottomed pond. When the pond was redesigned with a higher water level, the milestone was submerged.

Only one petrifying well, at the Aquarium on South Parade, now represents the many which once attracted visitors by the thousand. Everything imaginable was laid out under sprays of the heavily mineralised waters, to be gradually 'turned to stone': wigs, shoes, toys, human and other skulls, baskets of ferns, and birds' nests complete with eggs.

Lovers' Walks – initially laid out in the 1730s – follow the far banks of the Derwent, accessible from the Jubilee Bridge up-river but no longer reached by means of wire-operated ferries. A ferry near the Pavilion was the scene of a tragedy during the First World War when a Canadian soldier, stationed at the Royal Hotel, accepted a bet to haul himself across the wire hand-over-hand. Sadly, he lost his grip and fell in; his body was never recovered.

Lovers' Walks are seen to magical effect during the annual Matlock Bath Illuminations, with miles of coloured bulbs reflected in the Derwent. Decorated and illuminated boats glide along the river at weekends, their boatmen blending imperceptibly into the surrounding darkness. Seventy years ago a

water-powered switchback was the main attraction in the riverside Derwent Gardens. One 'well-known physician' recommended at least half-a-dozen rides for the benefit of one's liver. All good for business – at any rate the proprietor, Mr Buxton, often took his takings home in a wheelbarrow!

The riverside road, the A6, formerly connected with the Nottingham to Newhaven turnpike at Cromford, with two tollgates in the vicinity of Masson Mills. Built in 1783 as the showpiece

Masson Mills

mills of Sir Richard Arkwright, inventor of the water frame, these buildings now operate as a shopping village and working textile museum, with authentic machinery clattering away in rhythmic, almost deafening action. Families who have worked here for generations are still represented on the workforce.

Masson Mill is associated with the most unusual weir on the Derwent, unique for its downstream curve. Some years ago a photograph taken by Derbyshire's Frank Rodgers aroused a great deal of interest, including a letter from Canada pointing out that beavers always curve their dams downstream, which, said the writer, 'must prove something'. Brian Cooper, in *Transformation of a Valley*, muses that Arkwright feared the Derwent, having seen mills and bridges swept away by furious floods. Perhaps he reasoned that a convex weir would spread the worst of the force when the river was in spate.

The river continues to provide power to the building, no longer by a waterwheel but by means of a turbine plant which also supplies surplus electricity to the National Grid under the Non-Fossil Fuel Obligation.

Massive Surges of Water

Beyond Masson Mills the Derwent begins to curve away from the A6, flowing unhindered by Arkwright's Cromford Mill, powered during its working life by the waters of Bonsall Brook and Cromford Sough. Arkwright is known as 'father of the factory system' since his cotton mill successfully brought together an on-site workforce, machinery and, most importantly, a reliable water supply. The modest Bonsall Brook is at least on a par with the Derwent for carrying Britain into the Industrial Revolution.

The brook rises above the old village of Bonsall, where framework knitters' workshops survive from the days of small-scale hosiery production. Bonsall also has a fine market cross, yet never managed to acquire a market charter. The brook once ran alongside the main street, spanned by slabs of limestone in front of the cottages, until a local lady of means, Miss Prince, paid for the water to be culverted. And

thereby hangs a tale: a local lad went to seek his fortune in London, where he was mocked for his country ways until he let it be known that he came from a village where the houses were reached over marble bridges, and where lived princes.

Bonsall lead miners enjoyed the added reward of silver which occurred in the rich lead deposits of Ball Eye Mine. Other mineral riches have included calamine, barytes, china stone and fluorspar. A corn mill stood on Bonsall Brook from early times, with other ventures later established further downstream and along the Via Gellia. This pretty road was laid in 1791 by Philip Gell of Hopton, responsible for its rather grand, Latinised name. Over the years a succession of millponds, sturdy dam walls, culverts and weirs harnessed the waters to power a comb shop, lead smelters, slag grinding mill, paper mills, paintworks and sawmill. A cotton spinning mill produced the first Viyella – a contraction of Via Gellia.

Bonsall Brook flows down into Cromford, turning a restored over-shot waterwheel and feeding the picture-postcard millpond at Scarthin before disappearing underground en route for Arkwright's Cromford Mill. This historic mill complex is in the commendable hands of the Arkwright Society, which has rescued it from certain demolition and transformed the site into a world-famous visitor attraction.

Prominently sited above the left bank of the Derwent is Willersley Castle, built as a residence for Sir Richard Arkwright, but who died shortly before it was completed. The great man is laid to rest in St Mary's Church across the river. In 1919 a Roman pig of lead was found in the churchyard; the ancient Hereward Street is thought to have swung round to ford the Derwent near the present road bridge. A ruined medieval bridge chapel testifies to the perils faced by bygone travellers. In this little building and depending on their direction, they could pray for, or give thanks for, a safe crossing of the river. The chapel has 15th-century features, the same period attributed to the three pointed downstream arches of the bridge. The upstream arches are of later, rounded construction. An apparently unused fishing temple stands beside the chapel.

Leawood Pumphouse on the Cromford Canal

Our river has now run half its course. It next performs an occasional task at Leawood Pumphouse on the Cromford Canal. Completed in 1793, the canal really came into its own with the opening of the Cromford & High Peak Railway, transporting over 300,000 tons of canal freight in 1849 alone. However,

every time a barge entered or left the waterway, water was lost to the adjoining Erewash Canal via a series of locks. Action was needed to maintain water levels in the Cromford Canal and the answer was a mighty 70 h.p. steam engine, capable of raising almost 28 tons of water a minute from the Derwent below. Today the engine and boilers of Leawood Pumphouse are maintained by volunteers, and visitors can see the impressive sight of the pump in steam several times a year, topping up the canal with massive surges of water raised from the Derwent.

Leawood Pumphouse is a short towpath stroll from High Peak Junction workshops, repository of relics from the historic Cromford and High Peak Railway (CHPR), including several metres of 'fish-belly' rail, reputedly the oldest section of railway in the world. Weekends often see the blacksmith at work in his forge. Walkers and cyclists can follow the line of the old CHPR, now the High Peak Trail, a route full of interest even before it reaches the engine house at Middleton Top with its magnificent working engine.

En route and depending on the season, you can take in wonderful views from Black Rocks, ride into Killer's Dale on the quaint Steeple Grange narrow gauge railway and visit the National Stone Centre with its fossil-laden quarry trails and indoor exhibitions. We will each use some 20 lorry-loads of stone in our lifetime, in ways which are bound to come as a surprise to most. Out of doors the site offers evidence of volcanic activity, a Sea Lily Meadow and former tropical lagoons scattered with sharks' teeth. One of the quarries here was last worked to supply stone for the M1 motorway in the mid-1960s.

PART SIX

Cromford to the Amber Valley

Middleton Top has a car park and cycle hire centre, ideally sited for venturing out into the White Peak and a landscape far different from the Derwent Valley. Or there is Wirksworth to explore, an historic old market town boasting intimate links with quarrying and lead mining, the area memorably described by D. H. Lawrence as 'the navel of

England'. For a time Lawrence and his wife Frieda lived at Mountain Cottage perched above the Via Gellia. And George Eliot, whose real name was Mary Ann Evans, often stayed in Wirksworth at the home of her aunt, Elizabeth Evans, the inspiration for Dinah Morris in Eliot's *Adam Bede*.

In the not-so-distant past, Wirksworth was the nucleus of the largest tape producing centre in the world, specialising in the notorious red tape beloved of lawyers and civil servants. A mill on Gorsey Bank produced the fuse-binding tape of every Mills Bomb used in the First World War. Fascinating stories are revealed in Wirksworth Heritage Centre, housed in a former silk and velvet mill off the market place, where in 1788 a breeches-maker sold his wife to a shoemaker for 5s 3d (26p). Tuesday is still market day ...

A stream rising just south of Wirksworth is the infant river Ecclesbourne, set to join the Derwent at Duffield. Even this small river has had a working life, powering a sequence of mills including Speedwell, a tape mill. The route through the Ecclesbourne valley is quite beautiful. There was a time when charcoal

Middleton Top Engine House

Lea Hurst, Holloway

burners went about their business in the spinneys and copses, while clog-block cutters worked amongst alder trees growing thickly along the river banks. It was the cutters' job to saw and split alder logs into short blocks for despatch to clog makers, mainly in Lancashire and Yorkshire, where they were carved into shape and fitted with leather uppers ready for wear.

But to return to the Derwent where we last saw it, at High Peak Junction. Peeping out from Bow Wood east of the river is Castletop Farm, childhood home of writer Alison Uttley, creator of Little Grey Rabbit and prolific author of children's books.

Another famous lady was brought up at nearby Holloway, her name Florence Nightingale. Local tradition maintains that Florence first became interested in caring for others as a young girl, helping needy and sick villagers. Her old home, Lea Hurst, has for many years been a care home for the elderly but is currently under threat of closure. The presence of Miss Nightingale is felt strongly in this lovely house overlooking a deer park. Her bedroom contains personal belongings, from her desk to albums of pressed flowers, while her beloved pet owl, Athena – thanks to the skills of a Victorian taxidermist – bestows a glassy stare on residents and visitors alike.

Holloway's sister villages, Dethick and Lea, each have claims to fame. Dethick Manor was the family home of Anthony Babington, found guilty of treason in 1586 and hanged, drawn and quartered with gruesome severity on the direct orders of Queen Elizabeth I. It had been Babington's misfortune to play a major role in plotting to assassinate Elizabeth in order to bring Mary, Queen of Scots to the English throne. Alison Uttley drew on this story for her book *A Traveller in Time*.

The fortunes of Lea are inseparable from those of the famous Lea Mills, a textile factory built on the Lea Brook and still operating under the name of John Smedley, the hydropathic pioneer referred to earlier. In the early days of his experiments with the Mild Water Cure, Smedley treated his Lea Mills employees free of charge, apparently with considerable satisfaction all round. Today, John Smedley cottons and woollens are held in high regard, their classic black polo-neck jumpers favoured by the likes of Sean Connery and Omar Sharif.

Many Industrial Pies

Shortly below the point where Lea Brook joins the Derwent, the Meerbrook Sough – built in 1772 to drain lead mines in the Wirksworth area – still discharges millions of gallons of water a day into the river. The A6 has been west of the Derwent since Matlock, crossing back again at the curiously-named village of Whatstandwell, supposedly derived from the name of one Wat (Walter) Stonewell who lived near to where the first Whatstandwell Bridge was built six centuries ago. The local railway station is still in use, though a little further down the line from Florence Nightingale's day. There she alighted from the London train on

her return from the Crimea, without any fuss or advance notice to her housekeeper, to walk home alone across the fields.

No one seems to know how or why the admittedly bosky hamlet of Robin Hood got its name; just a few houses on a lane leading to Crich. Crich achieved passing fame as Cardale in the TV hit series *Peak Practice* and at its highest point gives us the magnificent landmark of Crich Stand, the Sherwood Foresters' Regimental Memorial, 63ft (19m) high with 58 steps to the viewing platform. At 950ft (290m) above sea-level the monument gives sweeping views into six counties and in turn is visible from many miles away, especially at night when its rotating searchlight beacon seems to wink out over the countryside.

Crich Stand looks down into the massive Cliffe Quarry, leased around 1840 by George Stephenson of *Rocket* and railway fame but a man with fingers in many industrial pies. Stephenson owned Clay Cross colliery and decided to make use of his low quality coal and slack by going into the lime burning business. He built 20 enormous kilns at Ambergate; though later changed in design they remained in use until 1965.

Stephenson's Kilns at Ambergate

Crich Tramway Village, overlooked by Crich Stand

terminus for scenic tram rides. Woodland walks pass large wooden sculptures including a Green Man and a dentally-challenged troll. The recent acquisition of a rare blue Police telephone box draws *Dr Who* fans from far and wide, coming to admire what they firmly believe to be a Tardis. So far it has not been seen to move of its own accord.

Down in the valley the river is fast approaching Ambergate, from where water is pumped to Carsington Reservoir whenever necessary. The reservoir was inaugurated in 1992 to help meet demand for water from Derbyshire, Nottinghamshire and Leicestershire. The siting of this artificial lake in such a glorious natural setting has created Carsington Water, a beauty spot attracting over half a million visitors a year. Dry land facilities include a visitor centre and shops, gentle walks and cycle tracks, while a water sports centre offers fishing, sailing, canoeing and windsurfing. The most intriguing man-made feature is Stones Island, lapped by the water and reached by a causeway. Its group of simple monoliths, up to 4 metres high, echoes the Derbyshire tradition of erecting stone monuments.

A long stretch of the Derwent beyond Whatstandwell Bridge is bordered by Shining Cliff Woods, once described by local schoolchildren as 'a beautiful name for a glorious hill, rosy in June with masses of rhododendrons'. These dense woods stretch all the way to Ambergate, where the Derwent embraces the River Amber after its journey through the pretty village of Ashover and the constraints of Ogston reservoir, often busy with sailing boats and always so with bird-watchers. The Amber also skirts Wingfield Park, where the ruins of Wingfield Manor sigh with memories of its royal captive, Mary, Queen of Scots, and tales of her secret and treasonable trysts with Anthony Babington, disguised as a Gypsy, his face stained with walnut juice.

By this time Crich Tramway Village had become firmly established in Cliffe Quarry. In this place of nostalgia and fascination, older visitors may recognise one imposing edifice as the facade of the old Derby Assembly Rooms, re-erected here stone by stone following redevelopment at Derby. It now overlooks a cobbled main street with pub and tea rooms, an Emporium recalling traditional sweet shops of mouth-watering memory, and, best of all, a

Carsington Water

Three other Derbyshire men from this stretch of the Amber Valley almost shared Babington's awful fate, already told, but over two centuries later. In 1817, a time of countrywide discontent, the White Horse Inn in sleepy little Pentrich became the headquarters of a conspiracy to overthrow the government. Labourers from Pentrich, Swanwick and Wingfield became embroiled in a plot to march on London. But they got no further than Kimberley in Nottinghamshire before they were waylaid and arrested by the 15th Hussars.

The ringleaders of this so-called Pentrich Revolution, James Brandreth, William Turner and Isaac Ludlam, were found guilty of the capital offence of High Treason and sentenced to be hanged, drawn and quartered at Derby.

This was the last time this sentence was pronounced. The drawing and quartering element was commuted but all three were hanged then beheaded on a block now in Derby Museum. Twenty of their followers were transported and the rest received a free pardon. The poet Shelley had witnessed the gory execution and under a nom-de-plume published an indignant pamphlet referring to 'the corpse of British liberty'. Such was 'England's last revolution'.

PART SEVEN

Amber Valley to Duffield

A gentler tale is revealed by taking a waymarked path through Shining Cliff Woods to Betty Kenny's Tree, the remains of an ancient yew. Betty was really called Kate Kenyon, and her husband Luke was a charcoal burner working these woods in the late 1700s. They actually lived out in the open beneath the spreading branches of the yew tree, probably adding a turf roof for shelter. The couple raised eight children in this poor hovel and the story goes that the babies were rocked to sleep in the springy branches of the yew. And so was born the nursery rhyme *Rock-a-Bye Baby*. Luke and Kate were still living in the tree at Luke's death – aged 96 – and his widow supposedly took part in a dance at Alderwasley Hall after her 100th birthday. The Betty Kenny Trail can be followed by entering the wood from Holly Lane, a side road just beyond the Hurt Arms Hotel at Ambergate.

The Hurt Arms may sound like some sort of painful pun but Hurt was the name of the Lords of the Manor of Alderwasley. Their seat was Alderwasley Hall and the Hurts were generous benefactors to nearby Crich, contributing to places of worship, the school and Crich Stand. In 1785 Francis Hurt replaced the original wooden viewing stand with the first of several stone towers. The family's many business operations included

Morley Park Ironworks, from which a pair of stone, flat-topped pyramids survive in a field beside the A38. These are the remains of two late 18th-century blast furnaces, the first in Derbyshire to burn charcoal instead of coke.

Another rare structure stands against the skyline east of Ambergate and Belper. This is Heage windmill, with her rare configuration of six sails. She (for windmills, like ships, are honorary females) was built in the late 1800s to replace a previous mill wrecked by a gale, and is the only remaining stone-towered, multi-sailed windmill in England. She ceased work at the end of the First World War, was restored as a visitor attraction in 2002, and is once more capable of grinding corn.

Belper is another settlement with a great debt to the Derwent. The town's five-storey North Mill is the second on this site. The first, built by Richard Arkwright and Jedediah Strutt – inventor of the Derby Rib, a machine for making ribbed stockings – was lost in a catastrophic uninsured fire. All cotton mill owners had an abiding dread of fire, a common disaster which drove many into financial ruin. The man who achieved fame for designing a fireproof mill was Jedediah's eldest son, William, an architect and gifted mechanic. His prototype was his father's second North Mill, rebuilt

A Gun Embrasure on Strutt's Bridge

bridge has gun embrasures intended as a defensive measure against attacks by the feared Luddites, responsible in the early 1800s for outbreaks of machine wrecking. Arkwright actually took the precaution of arming his Cromford Mill with 'Fifteen hundred Stand of small Arms ... a great Battery of Cannon' and 'upwards of 500 spears'. In the event, the Luddites descended on neither Strutt nor Arkwright. The barrel of one of Arkwright's cannons stands upright in the pavement outside Cromford Mill, with a cannon ball welded into its barrel.

Belper's North Mill houses the Derwent Valley Visitor Centre, while a short walk along the Ashbourne Road gives a fine view of the broad Horseshoe Weir with its ingenious flood controls. Construction of this weir created a 22-acre lake and at one time powered 11 wheels. But it is East Mill which dominates the scene. Seven stories high, it was built without external scaffolding, an amazing feat made possible by gangs of brave bricklayers who built ever upwards by leaning out from an internal steel frame.

using cast iron columns with transverse arches not of brick but of weight-saving hollow earthenware pots. At its completion in 1804, Strutt's mill was the most technically advanced building of its kind in the world.

The North Mill complex is connected to the even taller East Mill of 1912 by a low covered bridge spanning the Ashbourne Road. The

East Mill, Belper

Strutt's Horseshoe Weir and Flood Control Bridge, Belper

In all, Jedediah Strutt and his sons built eight mills at Belper and a further complex down river at Milford. They equipped their factories with remarkably advanced water control mechanisms, including the Horseshoe Weir mentioned above and a double weir serving their Milford site. As with Arkwright at Cromford, Jedediah Strutt built houses and facilities in Belper for his workers. Restored classic mill houses can be seen on the cobbled Long Row, a short walk from North Mill.

Lord Nelson's Vest

Prior to cotton spinning, the chief industry in Belper was nail making, first recorded here in 1313. Three hundred years ago the town was even exporting to the American colonies. Whole families lived and worked in their own smithy, often a cramped stone-built 'shop'. The work was so intolerably hot and stultifying that the nailers worked stripped to the waist – men, women and children side by side. Their raw material came in the form of rods of iron, forged in slitting mills as at Milford, Alderwasley and Derby – all of course on the Derwent. Some nailers' cottages have been restored but one small stone building on Joseph Street has, thankfully, not been prettified at all. Better still, an assortment of old nails is displayed in the window.

Workers' Housing on Long Row, Belper

29

Nailer's Shop on Joseph Street, Belper

In the lower part of town yet another brooding old mill enjoys modern life, now as the De Bradelei shopping outlet. As Brettles Hosiery Works the mill was famed for manufacturing the vest worn by Lord Nelson at Trafalgar, silk hose for King George III and the silk stockings worn by Queen Victoria for her coronation.

Lying westwards, in the fork between the Derwent and Ecclesbourne rivers, is Hazelwood, where everyday pottery was produced for Roman Britain; examples have been found as far north as Hadrian's Wall. East of Belper is the curiously named Denby Bottles, a literal link to the famous Denby Pottery, founded 200 years ago to utilise the local fireclays and still in business. We are in coal mining country now, at least this is what it

was until the collieries were closed down. If the ghost of David Herbert Lawrence – a miner's son – walked his native Eastwood now, he would hardly know the place. He might just recognise the two-up, two-down brick house where he was born, now a museum devoted to his life and works.

The Derwent, meanwhile, loops round to Milford and tumbles over Strutt's breathtaking double weir. George Stephenson had hoped to lay his North Midland Railway along this section of the valley but the Strutts, fearful for their water supply, put a spanner in his works. So a tunnel was driven through Chevin Hill with the help of a rotating alignment telescope mounted on the 50ft (15m) gritstone tower which still stands on the ridge of the Chevin.

On the east bank of the river between Milford and Little Eaton is Peckwash Paper Mill, built by Thomas Tempest in 1805. Calling on an existing medieval charter, Tempest was granted the right to extract water from the Derwent; he eventually had five large waterwheels operating what was claimed to be the biggest paper mill in England and maybe Europe. Its chimney, constructed when the waterwheels stopped turning in favour of steam turbines, fell into disuse in 1906 and has not smoked since.

The Double Weir at Milford

PART EIGHT

Duffield to Wilne

The proximity of the Derwent must have had some influence on the siting of Duffield Castle, built originally of wood by Henry de Ferrers in 1068. De Ferrers was a trusted kinsman of William the Conqueror and became one of the commissioners who helped to compile his Domesday Survey. The wooden castle was rebuilt in stone after about 100 years, a massive construction with a 95ft x 93ft (29 x 28.3m) keep and walls 15ft (4.5m) thick. A further century on, Duffield Castle was the stronghold of Robert de Ferrers, 6th Earl of Derby, the most rebellious of the barons who in opposing Henry III took England to the brink of civil war. Ferrers had already received one conditional pardon but then re-armed his men, probably rallying his followers from Duffield Castle. Royal troops swiftly descended on Derbyshire, clashing with the rebel forces at the Battle of Chesterfield. Ferrers was captured, according to legend through the treachery of a woman, and Duffield Castle was razed to the ground. After three years in prison Ferrers was freed to return to Derbyshire but all he had left of his family's once extensive estates was a portion at Holbrook.

Duffield Castle was probably the third largest in the country after the Tower of London and Colchester. Today the site is owned by the National Trust and accessed via a flight of steps beside the A6, but there is little to see other than a capped well. Derby Museum has evidence of Roman and Anglo-Saxon occupation of the site, along with a bucket recovered from the well.

Modern bridges span the Derwent on its way to Darley Abbey, where once stood a 12th-century Augustinian monastery. Robert de Ferrers and other prominent landowners gave generously to the monastery, not just for prestige but to curry favour from above when their time came. Gifts came from the moderately wealthy too: rental income from Alvaston Mill paid for sacramental wine, revenues from land at Youlgreave provided the canons with shoes and clothing. Even fishing rights on the Derwent belonged to the Abbot of Darley, leased out to individuals at an annual rent of two shillings.

Darley Abbey became the richest and most powerful in Derbyshire with property encompassing numerous churches and chapels, a dozen manors and land in over 30 towns and villages. Commercial life extended around the county with interests in large-scale sheep farming and wool production, arable farming, forestry and – to the abbey's great good fortune – minerals. At the dissolution of the monasteries Darley Abbey reportedly owned a

hoard of pigs of lead worth several tens of thousands of pounds. No amount of wealth could prevent the destruction of the abbey in 1538, except for what may have been the guest house, now The Abbey Inn.

An assortment of small businesses now occupies the old Darley Abbey Cotton Mill,

established by Thomas Evans in 1783 on the east bank of the Derwent. Only the mill-wheel could be salvaged when the first building burned down. Fortunately the mill was insured and the present building was up and running within a year. Across the river the Evanses built a factory village of nearly 200 dwellings, many now restored as very desirable properties. Village and factory were, and still are, connected by a toll-bridge over the Derwent which even today's travellers may have to pay a charge to cross.

Down river lies Little Chester, Derby's oldest suburb, with its history of complete isolation in times of flood. Markeaton Brook shares the blame with the Derwent for some of the worst floods; that of 1932 is still fresh in local memory.

Darley Abbey Mill

Opposite: The Abbey Inn

Above: The Abbey Inn sign

Little Chester was the Roman fort of Derventio, meaning 'many oak trees' and the derivation of the name of our river. A timber-built fort was constructed in the reign of the Emperor Nero to guard this important river crossing. It stood in what is now Strutt's Park but was superseded by a larger fort on lower ground. Roy Christian describes Little Eaton as 'an area where Roman artefacts are as numerous as weeds in a warm, wet summer'. The river itself has given up secrets of the Roman occupation, including submerged bridge foundations to suggest that the Old Chester Road, which now ends at the river, used to be carried over and onwards.

Archaeologists have found evidence of kilns and hearths from the working of iron, pottery and lead, though visible remains of domestic life are scant – a couple of wells, masonry and a few foundation stones. Traces of the Derventio bath house could be seen before being buried beneath Parker's Piece playing fields. Little

Chester honours its Roman inheritance in such names as Caesar Street, Centurion Walk and Derventio Close.

Heads and Quarters

Riverside paths in central Derby are full of interest. St Mary's Bridge Chapel is one of only six English medieval bridge chapels used for regular worship. With a history traceable to the 13th century and restored about 70 years ago, the chapel served the same purpose as the one on Cromford Bridge (see Part 5). During the reign of Bloody Mary three Catholic priests, known as the Padley Martyrs, were hanged, drawn and quartered on St Mary's Bridge, their heads and quarters afterwards impaled on spikes around the town. An annual commemoration service is held each July at Padley Chapel near Hathersage.

Derby's Silk Mill Industrial Museum is the southern boundary of the Derwent Valley Mills World Heritage Site. Thomas Cotchett constructed the mill in 1704 on the By-Flatt, a narrow island in the Derwent. Powered by a 13ft 6in (4m) waterwheel, the machinery was installed by George Sorocold, who had earlier constructed Derby's first public waterworks. This ingenious system was powered by a waterwheel which pumped water from the Derwent to a holding tank in St Michael's churchyard, carried by means of pipes made from bored tree trunks. The water was available only to subscribers and the system worked for a century-and-a-half. The brilliant Sorocold went on to design similar utilities for other towns and cities, not least the London Bridge waterworks.

Cotchett's venture, meanwhile, had failed and been taken over by Thomas and John Lombe. The Lombes had resorted to a dangerous trip to Italy and a touch of industrial espionage to steal jealously guarded production secrets. With Sorocold as their engineer, they set about massive expansion using Italian-style

Bonnie Prince Charlie, gazing forever southwards

Charles spent the night at Lord Exeter's House in Full Street but then came news that the feared Duke of Cumberland was leading an army to intercept the rebels. By 6 December they were in retreat, to the jeers of a rather relieved populace. The bedraggled Scots, now hungry and footsore, were preceded by rumours of their wild, uncivilised behaviour, and Peakland farmers hid their livestock in the hills and lowered their valuables – including a grandfather clock – down lead mine shafts.

The relentless Cumberland crushed the cause of the Stuarts forever at the bloody Battle of Culloden in April 1746.

Derby has a continuing regal connection in the name of its famous Royal Crown Derby porcelain, founded by William Duesbury in 1755 near old St Mary's Bridge. This company is the oldest surviving manufacturer of English porcelain and enjoys a worldwide export market.

Leaving central Derby, the Derwent passes beneath road and rail bridges to execute a series of loops, encircling two man-made lakes in a nature reserve that attracts an enormous variety of birds. Unfurled again for its last few

machinery. More than 94,000 moving parts were motivated from a single source of water power. Their operation was a great success and silk became Derby's main industry, with a dozen silk mills in production by 1789.

From the riverside lawns outside the silk mill a man on horseback gazes forever southwards. This bronze statue is 'Bonnie Prince Charlie', the handsome Young Pretender who got no further than Swarkestone Bridge on his ill-fated bid for the Crown in 1745. Marching south from Scotland with London their goal, Charles Edward Stuart and 'great numbers' of his followers reached Ashbourne, where on 4 December the Prince was proclaimed King in the market place. His vanguard reached Derby later that same day, gratified to find that His Worship the Mayor, along with the good magistrates and hundreds of men raised to defend the town, had fled.

Wilne Mill